New England's
Lighthouses
A Photographic Portrait

Jean Patey

First published in the United States
of America by:

Twin Lights Publishers, Inc.
10 Hale Street
Rockport, Massachusetts 01966
Telephone: (978) 546-7398
http://www.twinlightspub.com

ISBN 1-885435-50-9

10 9 8 7 6 5 4 3 2 1

(*right*)

Pemaquid Point Light
Entrance to Muscongus Bay and John Bay,
Bristol, Maine
PHOTO: WILLIAM A. BRITTEN

Cover::
Point Gammon Light
Massachusetts
PHOTO: BRIAN TAGUE

Text by:
Jean Patey

Book design by
SYP Design & Production, Inc.
http://www.sypdesign.com

Printed in China

Contents

INTRODUCTION

From the early 17th century, British colonies began to dot the rugged New England coast. As colonial populations grew, so did trade along the coastline and with European merchants. Finding safe and dependable trade routes proved a formidable task. The roadways connecting the fledgling towns were practically non-existent, making travel arduous. Oceanic trade established itself as the preferred means of transporting goods. At the same time, the New England seashore presented a distinct set of problems. Miles of rugged shoals, numerous offshore islands, and powerful currents left mariners uncertain as to whether the waters they navigated were safe for passage. A lighting system to safely guide ships along the coastlines and through harbor entrances became imperative.

In 1716 King George I authorized the first American lighthouse to be built. Nearly a dozen lighthouses spanned the coast by the end of the British rule. After the colonies gained their independence, the new government appointed the lighthouse keepers. These people didn't undergo special training for the lives that they were committing themselves to. They were ordinary civilians who found themselves drawn to the sea.

The lives of lighthouse keepers are painted with a rich history of dedication, courage, and heroism. The keepers were souls committed to the duty of assuring that no ship would blindly run aground on their watch. This meant keeping the lights in the lighthouse lit, even as hurricane driven waves thundered down upon their shores and buildings. They refused to abandon their obligation to watch over the lights until the storm passed, even when the storm's breakers had swept away a loved one. When ships inevitably ran aground, keepers would charge out into perilous and stormy nights to rescue the stranded sailors. The safety and welfare of ships traveling along the coast was dependant upon the lighthouses, just as the well being of the lighthouses rested solely in the hands of the keepers. The keepers' responsibilities kept their lives centered on the lighthouse with an eye always on the horizon.

The automation of lighthouses and subsequent elimination of their caretakers has brought the tradition of the lighthouse keepers to its end, along with a chapter in America's maritime history. Lighthouses still possess a charm and allure that sparks an interest in people from all walks of life. This interest has seeded passionate efforts to rescue them from extinction and keep their lights shining. The Maine Lights Program, conceived by the Island Institute and legislated by Congress, led to the transfer of 28 lighthouse properties from the U.S. Coast Guard to nonprofit and government entities in 1998. Under the National Historic Lighthouse Preservation Act of 2000, more lighthouses are being turned over to qualified stewards. Two very successful Maine organizations, the American Lighthouse Foundation and *Lighthouse Digest Magazine*, along with various non-profit organizations, have formed to aid in the preservation of these beacons of safety.

New England's Lighthouses: A Photographic Portrait captures the essence of each and every existing lighthouse in New England. Immerse yourself in these photographs and understand the lighthouse magic that captures the hearts and minds of so many.

Boston Light
Little Brewster Island, Boston Harbor

PHOTO: BRIAN TAGUE

Maine

Marshall Point Lighthouse was erected in 1832 to aid mariners into Port Clyde Harbor. The existing lighthouse replaced the original lighthouse in 1857. The St. George Historical Society restored the house in 1990 and under the Maine Lights Program the entire station become the property of the town of St. George in 1998. The second floor apartment is privately occupied. The lighthouse and grounds are accessible year-round with the museum open from May to October.

Portland Breakwater Light was originally an octagonal wooden tower built in 1855. After the breakwater was extended in the early 1870's, the tower was moved to Little Diamond Island and used as a lookout tower. The present tower was built in 1875 at the end of the breakwater and is known locally as "Bug Light". In 1942 the light was extinguished and the property was sold. In 1985 it was donated to the city of South Portland and in 2002, after being restored, it was relit.

Boon Island, located off the coast of York, is surrounded by dangerous ledges. Three lighthouses were erected before the present light was constructed and activated in 1855. Severe weather constantly threatened lighthouse keepers and it was finally automated in 1978. It was licensed to the American Lighthouse Foundation in 2000.

Portland Head Light
Cape Elizabeth

PHOTO: BRIAN TAGUE

Portland Head Light, built in 1791, is the oldest lighthouse in Maine and considered by many to be the most spectacular lighthouse in New England. The present Victorian keeper's house was built in 1891 and replaced the original 1816 dwelling. The station was automated in 1989 and turned over to the town of Cape Elizabeth. In 1992 the keeper's house was opened as the Museum at Portland Head Light.

Saddleback Ledge Light
Isle au Haut Bay, Vinalhaven

PHOTO: © 2000 GARY P. RICHARDSON

Saddleback Ledge Light, built in 1839, is located
between Vinalhaven and Isle au Haut at the
entrance to the East Penobscot Bay. It was considered one of the most difficult stations to man, as it
is perched upon a bare rock with little vegetation.
It was automated in 1954 and subsequently the
Coast Guard destroyed the keeper's house around
1960. The lighthouse is not open to the public.

Cape Neddick
Off Cape Neddick, York

PHOTO: BERT GUERIN

Built in 1879, Cape Neddick Light, or Nubble
Light, is located on Nubble Island, just off Cape
Neddick. The light was automated in 1987 and
later became the property of the town of York
under the Maine Lights Program. With its 1928
fourth order Fresnel lens, the light continues to be
maintained by the Coast Guard. The grounds are
not open to the public but may be seen from
Sohier Park.

(top and bottom, left)

Doubling Point Light and Doubling Point Range Lights
Arrowsic Island, Kennebec River

TOP PHOTO: © RICHARD ASARISI
BOTTOM LEFT PHOTO: FRANCINE DOLLINGER

The Doubling Point Light and Range Lights were built in 1898 on the Kennebec River to aid mariners navigating the busy river. A year later the Doubling Point Light was moved offshore to a stone pier connected to shore by a footbridge. In 1935 the keeper's house was sold to a private owner.

In 1988 the Doubling Point Light was automated and two years later the Range Lights were automated. In 1998 Doubling Point Light was transferred to the Friends of Doubling Point Light and the Range Lights were transferred to the Range Light Keepers under the Maine Lights Program.

(bottom, right)

Halfway Rock Light
Casco Bay, near South Harpswell

PHOTO: THE LIGHTHOUSE PEOPLE
BOB AND SANDRA SHANKLIN

Halfway Rock Light, built in 1871, is located in Casco Bay some ten miles from Portland Head and is surrounded by treacherous ledges. Halfway Rock was a difficult post for keepers as it required an 11-mile row to Portland to obtain supplies. In 1975 Halfway Rock Light was automated and in 2000 it was licensed to the American Lighthouse Foundation.

Goat Island Light
Goat Island, Cape Porpoise Harbor, Kennebunkport

PHOTO: ROBERT A. DENNIS

Goat Island Light was built in 1833 to lead mariners
into Cape Porpoise Harbor, near the mouth of the
Kennebunk River. The present lighthouse was built
in 1859. In 1992 Goat Island was leased to the
Kennebunkport Conservation Trust and in 1998,
under the Maine Lights Program, it became the
property of that trust. The grounds and lighthouse
are open by special arrangement.

(above east and opposite west)

Cape Elizabeth Lights
Entrance to Casco Bay

PHOTOS: © RICHARD ASARISI

A pyramidal stone marker was erected at this site in 1811 to mark the
entrance to Portland Harbor. It was replaced in 1827 by a pair of stone
lighthouses, the first "twin" lights in Maine. In 1874 the present sixty-
seven-foot cast iron towers replaced the original towers. In 1924 the west
light was discontinued, and sold in 1959 to the highest bidder. The east
light was automated in 1963 and remains an active aid to navigation. The
lighthouse was licensed by the Coast Guard to the American Lighthouse
Foundation in 2000, while the keeper's house is privately owned.

Marty took me up for a view !

(top)

Bass Harbor Head Light
Mount Desert Island

PHOTO: RICK TOTTON

Bass Harbor Head Light sits high on a cliff on the southwestern side of Mount Desert Island. Built in 1858, it marks the entrance to Bass Harbor and Blue Hill Bay. The lighthouse was automated in 1974 and its 1902 fourth order Fresnel lens is in use today. The keeper's house is now occupied by a Coast Guard officer and the grounds are open to the public.

(bottom, left)

Squirrel Point Light
Arrowsic Island, Kennebec River

PHOTO: BERT GUERIN

Squirrel Point Light is an octagonal wood tower located on the eastern side of the Kennebec River. It is the second of four lights encountered on the river en-route to Bath. In 1998 ownership of the station was transferred to a non-profit organization.

(bottom, right)

Deer Island Thorofare Light
Mark Island, Deer Island Thorofare, Stonington

PHOTO: © 2000 ANNA P. KLEIN

Deer Island Thorofare Light, also known as Mark Island Light, is located in the Deer Island Thorofare in Penobscot Bay. Between 1959 and the 1970's the Coast Guard demolished the station but preserved the lighthouse. In 1998 ownership of the light was transferred to the Island Heritage Trust with the Coast Guard maintaining the light. Today, the trust maintains the island as a wildlife refuge where bald eagles and nesting eider ducks are found.

Sequin Island Light
off mouth of Kennebec River, near Popham Beach,
Georgetown

PHOTO: © KRAIG ANDERSON

The original Sequin Island Light, built in 1795, was
a wooden tower. The present tower was built in
1857. It is the highest elevated lighthouse in Maine
and the only lighthouse north of Rhode Island with
a first order Fresnel lens. The Friends of Sequin
Island was founded in 1989 after the lighthouse was
automated and the property was later transferred to
them in 1998 under the Maine Lights Program.

Burnt Island Light
Boothbay Harbor

PHOTO: BRIAN TAGUE

Burnt Island Light was erected in 1821 on the west side of Boothbay Harbor. In 1998, as part of the Maine Lights Program, ownership of the lighthouse was transferred to the Maine Department of Marine Resources. In 2003, after much hard work, the lighthouse was opened as "Burnt Island Living Lighthouse," providing insight into the lives of the keepers and their families as well as maritime history. Summer tours are offered daily.

Cuckolds Light
Approach to Boothbay Harbor

PHOTO: WILLIAM A. BRITTEN

The Cuckolds Light was built in 1892 on a small island off of Southport Island. It marks the entrance to Boothbay Harbor. In 1907 a small light tower was added to the roof of the original fog signal station to reduce the number of wrecks in the area. The light is maintained by the Coast Guard and is not open to the public.

(top)

West Quoddy Head Light
West Quoddy Head, Bay of Fundy, Lubec

PHOTO: JEREMY D'ENTREMONT

West Quoddy Head Light, with its famous red and white stripes, stands at the easternmost point of the United States. The stripes were added after the original tower of 1808 was replaced in 1858. At that time it received a third order Fresnel lens and a Victorian keeper's house. In 1998, it was transferred to the State of Maine and became part of Quoddy Head State Park. The visitor's center is maintained by the West Quoddy Head Light Keepers Association.

(bottom)

Hendricks Head Light
Sheepscot River Entrance, West Southport

PHOTO: WILLIAM BRITTEN

Hendricks Head Light stands at the entrance to the Sheepscot River. Originally the lighthouse was a granite structure with a tower situated on its roof. That building was replaced in 1875 with the current lighthouse and keeper's house. The lighthouse was deactivated in 1933, then sold privately. In 1951 it was relit when boating traffic increased. Today the lighthouse remains privately owned with the Coast Guard maintaining the light.

(opposite)

Dice Head Light
Mouth of the Penobscot River, Castine

PHOTO: SCOTT R. THORP

The Dice (or Dyce) Head Light was built in 1829 to mark the entrance to the Penobscot River and also Castine Harbor. In 1935 the light was discontinued and replaced with a skeletal tower. In 1937 the keeper's house and surrounding buildings went to the town of Castine. It wasn't until 1956 that the light itself was given to the town. Today the keeper's house is rented as a private residence.

(top)

Libby Island Light
Machias Bay entrance, Machiasport

PHOTO: THE LIGHTHOUSE PEOPLE
BOB AND SANDRA SHANKLIN

Libby Island Light, built in 1822, stands on Libby Island, which is actually two islands connected by a sandbar. After being automated in 1974 most of the buildings were destroyed. Under the Maine Lights Program the lighthouse was transferred to the U.S. Fish and Wildlife Service. The U. S. Coast Guard continues to maintain the light itself.

(bottom)

Great Duck Island Light
Blue Hill Bay Approach, Frenchboro

PHOTO: JEREMY D'ENTREMONT

Great Duck Island Light stands on a 265-acre island guiding mariners to the Mount Desert and Blue Hill Bay area. Most of the island was purchased in 1984 by the Maine Chapter of the Nature Conservancy. The light station became the property of Bar Harbor's College of the Atlantic under the Maine Lights Program. It is believed that 20% of Maine's nesting seabirds are on Great Duck Island. Lighthouse and grounds are not open to the public.

Owl's Head Light
Entrance to Rockland Harbor, Owl's Head

PHOTO: WILLIAM A. BRITTEN

Owl's Head Light stands only 30 feet tall atop a high bluff on the southern tip of Rockland Harbor. The lighthouse was automated in 1989 and its 1856 fourth order Fresnel lens is still in use today. The keeper's house is a Coast Guard residence with the surrounding area designated as a state park.

Two Bush Island Light
Two Bush Channel, near Spruce Head

PHOTO: © KRAIG ANDERSON

Two Bush Island Light, a square white brick tower, marks the entrance to Two Bush Channel. After being automated in 1964, the Green Berets destroyed the keeper's house in a demolition exercise. In 1998, under the Maine Lights Program, the lighthouse was transferred to the U.S. Fish and Wildlife Service.

Franklin Island Light
Franklin Island, Muscongus Bay, near Friendship

PHOTO: © KRAIG ANDERSON

Franklin Island Light, the third lighthouse in Maine, was built in 1807 to direct mariners away from the rocks of Franklin Island. The present lighthouse was built in 1855. After being automated in 1933 the station, except for the lighthouse, was demolished. The lighthouse is now a national wildlife refuge and is cared for by Franklin Light Preservation, Inc. under a contract with the Coast Guard.

Monhegan Island Light
Monhegan Island

PHOTO: WILLIAM A. BRITTEN

Monhegan Island Light is located ten-miles off the coast of Maine. It was built in 1824 and was replaced in 1850 by the existing structure. In 1962 the Monhegan Associates purchased the grounds and buildings, excluding the lighthouse. The property was transferred to the Monhegan Historical and Cultural Museum Association in 1998 under the Maine Lights Program. The 1857 assistant keeper's house has since been rebuilt and is used as an art museum. The U. S. Coast Guard maintains the lighthouse.

(top)

Indian Island Light
Rockport Harbor, Penobscot Bay, Rockport

PHOTO: © KRAIG ANDERSON

Indian Island Light, originally built in 1850, is located at the entrance to Rockport Harbor, home of the famous Andre the Seal. Use of the lighthouse was discontinued in 1856 and not reactivated until 1875 when the present lighthouse was built. When an automatic light was placed on Lowell Rock in 1934 the light was permanently deactivated and sold to a private party.

(bottom, left)

Grindle Point Light
Islesboro Island, Islesboro

PHOTO: © 2000 GARY P. RICHARDSON

Grindle Point Light was built in 1851 on Islesboro Island to direct mariners entering Gilkey Harbor. It was rebuilt in 1874 after falling into disrepair and later deactivated in 1934. A skeletal tower was placed nearby. The town of Islesboro purchased the lighthouse and grounds and the keeper's house was converted into a museum. At the request of the local citizens, the light was moved back to the lighthouse in 1987 and the skeleton tower was removed.

(bottom, right)

Wood Island Light
Wood Island, mouth of the Saco River, near Biddeford

PHOTO: JEREMY D'ENTREMONT

Wood Island Light is located on the northeast side of Wood Island Harbor, signaling the entrance to the Saco River. The original lighthouse of 1808 was rebuilt in 1839 and again in 1858. In 1970 twenty-eight acres were deeded to the Maine Audubon Society. In 2003 the lighthouse was licensed to the American Lighthouse Foundation and is cared for by one of its chapters, the Friends of Wood Island Lighthouse.

Curtis Island Light
Curtis Island, Camden

PHOTO: © RICHARD ASARISI

Curtis Island Light was built in 1835 on what was then called Negro Island to aid mariners into Camden Harbor. The present lighthouse was built in 1896. In 1934 the island was renamed Curtis Island after Cyrus Curtis, publisher of the *Saturday Evening Post.* In 1972 the light was automated and later turned over to the town of Camden in 1998 under the Maine Lights Program. The island is a public park while the Coast Guard maintains the light.

Nash Island Light
Nash Island, Southeast mouth of Pleasant Bay, Addison

PHOTO: JEREMY D'ENTREMONT

Nash Island Light was built in 1838 to mark the opening of Pleasant River. The original wooden structure was replaced with the existing structure in 1873. In 1947 the Coast Guard destroyed all the buildings except the lighthouse. It was decommissioned in 1982 and replaced with an offshore buoy. Under the Maine Lights Program the lighthouse was turned over to the Friends of Nash Island Light in 1998 and is undergoing restoration.

Rockland Breakwater Light
Rockland

PHOTO: BERT GUERIN

In 1902 the Rockland Breakwater Light was erected. After it was automated in 1965 it fell into disrepair and the Coast Guard planned to destroy it. Instead the Samoset Resort took responsibility for a portion of the upkeep until 1989. Under the Maine Lights Program it was transferred to the city of Rockland in 1998 and they, in turn, lease it to the Friends of Rockland Breakwater Lighthouse, a chapter of the American Lighthouse Foundation.

Rockland Harbor Southwest Light
Rockland

PHOTO: © MARILYN STIBOREK

The Rockland Harbor Southwest Light, built in 1987, is the youngest lighthouse in Maine and the only one to be privately constructed. The Coast Guard was convinced to recognize the light as an official aid to navigation since it indicates the hazard at Seal Ledge.

Pond Island Light
Pond Island, mouth of the Kennebec River,
Georgetown

PHOTO: © RICHARD ASARISI

Pond Island Light is sited at the entrance to the
Kennebec River, just off of Popham Beach. The
original lighthouse was built in 1821 and replaced
with the present lighthouse in 1855. In 1963 The
Coast Guard destroyed all of the station's buildings
except for the newly automated lighthouse, which it
continues to maintain. The island is now the Pond
Island National Wildlife Refuge, managed by the
U.S. Fish and Wildlife Service

(top)

Moose Peak Light
Mistake Island, Jonesport

PHOTO: THE LIGHTHOUSE PEOPLE
BOB AND SANDRA SHANKLIN

Moose Peak Light was built in 1827 on the east point of Mistake Island, one of the foggiest locations in Maine. The present tower was constructed in 1851. After being automated in 1972, the keeper's house was used for a military training exercise and destroyed in 1982. Today the lighthouse is maintained by the U.S. Coast Guard.

(bottom, left)

Baker Island Light
Cranberry Isles

PHOTO: THE LIGHTHOUSE PEOPLE
BOB AND SANDRA SHANKLIN

Baker Island, southeast of Mount Desert Island, is one of five islands that make up the Cranberry Isles. Baker Island Light, built in 1828, marks the entrance to Frenchman Bay. The present lighthouse was built in 1855, automated in 1966, and replaced by an offshore buoy in 2002. Today the Coast Guard maintains the lighthouse while Acadia National Park maintains other buildings on the site. The lighthouse is not open to the public.

(bottom, right)

Ladies Delight Light
Lake Cobbosseecontee, Manchester

PHOTO: THE LIGHTHOUSE PEOPLE
BOB AND SANDRA SHANKLIN

Ladies Delight Light was built in 1908 to aid in the navigation of a passenger boat on Lake Cobbosseecontee. The light is located on a jagged reef about a mile south of Island Park in Manchester. The light was erected by the Cobbosseecontee Yacht Club and continues to be maintained by its members.

Narraguagus Light
Pond Island, Narraguagus Bay, Milbridge

PHOTO: THE LIGHTHOUSE PEOPLE
BOB AND SANDRA SHANKLIN

Known by locals as Pond Island Light,
Narraguagus Light was built in 1853 on Pond
Island to mark the entrance to the harbor of
Milbridge. When the lighthouse was deactivated in
1934 it was sold and remains privately owned.

(top)

Prospect Harbor Point Light
Prospect Harbor Point, Prospect Harbor

Prospect Harbor Light signals the entrance to the harbor from the tip of Prospect Harbor Point. It was built in 1850 but was deactivated from 1859 to 1870 due to decreased trade. The present lighthouse was built in 1891 and today is part of a U.S. Naval Communications Center. The American Lighthouse Foundation maintains the lighthouse.

(bottom, left)

Brown's Head Light
Northwest end of Vinalhaven Island, Vinalhaven

Brown's Head Light, originally built in 1832, guides mariners through the western entrance to the Fox Islands Thorofare. The present lighthouse was erected in 1857. The lighthouse buildings were transferred in 1998 to the town of Vinalhaven where the town manager now resides. The Coast Guard maintains the light.

(bottom, right)

Blue Hill Bay Light
Green Island, Blue Hill Bay, Brooklin

Located on the west side of Green Island, the Blue Hill Bay Light, built in 1857, was once called Eggemoggin Lighthouse as it helped to guide mariners into Eggemoggin Reach. In 1933 use of the lighthouse was discontinued and it was replaced with a skeleton tower in 1935. Blue Hill Bay Light is now privately owned.

Heron Neck Light
Greens Island, entrance to Hurricane Sound,
Vinalhaven

PHOTO: © 2000 ANNA P. KLEIN

Heron Neck Light, built in 1854 on Greens Island,
is situated at the east entrance to Hurricane Sound
as an aid to mariners making their way to Carver's
Harbor. After a fire damaged the keeper's house in
1989 the Coast Guard planned to raze the building. After much objection, the lighthouse station
was leased to the Island Institute in Rockland and
restored by a private individual. Today it is used as
a research facility.

(left)

Ram Island Light
Fisherman's Passage, Ram Island, Boothbay Harbor

PHOTO: WILLIAM A. BRITTEN

Ram Island Light, located off the coast of Ocean Point, was built in 1883 and marks the entrance to Boothbay Harbor. It was automated in 1965 and the keeper's house was slated to be destroyed in 1983. Under the Maine Lights Program, it was transferred to the Grand Banks Schooner Museum Trust and is cared for by the Ram Island Preservation Society. Caretakers live on the island in the summer and the Coast Guard maintains the light.

(top, right) Seen it all my life

Ram Island Ledge Light
Portland Harbor, Casco Bay, Cape Elizabeth

PHOTO: JEREMY D'ENTREMONT

Ram Island Ledge Light sits on rocky ground at the northern entrance to Portland Harbor and was built in 1905. At high tide the ledge is completely covered, which made construction difficult. The lighthouse can be seen in the distance from Fort Williams State Park, the location of Portland Head Light.

(bottom, right)

Lubec Channel Light
Lubec Channel, Lubec

PHOTO: © RICHARD ASARISI

Lubec Channel Light, built in 1890, is situated at the western entrance to Lubec Channel. The US Coast Guard continues to maintain the light after almost discontinuing it in 1989.

(top)

Mount Desert Rock Light
About 25 miles from Bar Harbor

PHOTO: JEREMY D'ENTREMONT

Mount Desert Rock is a remote island located about twenty miles south of Mount Desert Island. The original lighthouse was built in 1830 to mark the entrance to Frenchman Bay and Blue Hill Bay. The present tower was built in 1847. It was automated in 1977 and leased to the College of the Atlantic where it became the summer base for Allied Whale, their marine mammal division. The college acquired the station in 1998.

(bottom)

Eagle Island Light
Eagle Island, East Penobscot Bay, Deer Isle

PHOTO: © RICHARD ASARISI

Eagle Island Light was built in 1838 to serve mariners sailing the Penobscot Bay. Eagle Island Light was automated in 1959. In 1964 the Coast Guard demolished all the buildings except the bell tower and the lighthouse. In 1998, under the Maine Lights Program, the lighthouse was transferred to the Eagle Island Caretakers. The lighthouse and grounds are not open to the public and the Coast Guard maintains the light.

(top)

Whaleback Light
Mouth of Piscataqua River, Kittery

PHOTO: ROSS TRACY

Whaleback Light is a conical granite tower situated in Maine waters and marks the approach to Portsmouth Harbor, New Hampshire. The first light was constructed in 1831, however, this light-house was poorly built and was replaced with the current dovetailed granite tower in 1872. During construction of this lighthouse the old tower remained standing. Its base is still visible today.

(bottom, left)

Spring Point Ledge Light
West Side of Portland Harbor

PHOTO: ROSS TRACY

Spring Point Ledge Light, built in 1897, is a brick "sparkplug" style tower which originally sat on a dangerous ledge at the west side of the Portland Harbor shipping channel. In 1951 a 900-foot breakwater was built, connecting the lighthouse to the mainland. In 1998 the Spring Point Ledge Light Trust obtained ownership of the light. The Portland Harbor Museum manages the site while the Coast Guard maintains the light itself. The lighthouse is occasionally opened.

(bottom, right)

Fort Point Light
Mouth of the Penobscot River, Stockton Springs

PHOTO: BERT GUERIN

Fort Point Light was built in 1836 on the west side of the Penobscot River to aid mariners bound for Bangor. The first light was a granite tower, which was replaced in 1857 with the current light. In 1998 the light was conveyed to the State of Maine Bureau of Parks and is managed by Fort Point State Historic Site. The light itself, with an 1857 fourth order Fresnel lens, continues to be maintained by the Coast Guard.

Pumpkin Island Light
Eggemoggin Reach, Penobscot Bay, Little Deer Island

PHOTO: SCOTT R. THORP

Pumpkin Island Light was established in 1854 to mark the entrance to Eggemoggin Reach. The light was automated in 1930 and in 1934 it was sold. It has remained privately owned.

Winter Harbor Light
Mark Island, Winter Harbor

PHOTO: SCOTT R. THORP

Winter Harbor Light, built in 1856, is located on Mark Island in Frenchman Bay. In 1934 the light was taken out of service and a lighted buoy was placed to the southeast. The lighthouse was sold and has remained privately owned.

Bear Island Light
Bear Island, Northeast Harbor

PHOTO: © 1996 GARY P. RICHARDSON

Bear Island Lighthouse, located near Northeast Harbor, marks the channel to Somes Sound, the only fjord on the east coast of the United States. Originally built in 1839, it was replaced with a brick lighthouse in 1889. It was deactivated from 1981 to 1989 and replaced by an offshore buoy. In 1989 it was restored and relit by the Friends of Acadia. The lighthouse is now leased by the National Park Service as a private residence.

Little River Light
Little River Island, Cutler

PHOTO: BILL COLLETTE, AMERICAN LIGHTHOUSE
FOUNDATION

Little River Light, built in 1847, stands on Little
River Island, near Cutler Harbor, which is the last
protected harbor south of Canada. The present
1876 structure was automated in 1975 and was
replaced in 1980 by a skeletal tower. It was licensed
to the American Lighthouse Foundation in 2000,
and relit in 2001. Ownership has now been transferred to the American Lighthouse Foundation. It
is not open to the public.

Egg Rock Light
Entrance to Frenchman Bay, Winter Harbor

PHOTO: FRANCINE DOLLINGER

Built in 1875 on a mass of ledges, Egg Rock Light
marks the entrance to Frenchman Bay and Bar
Harbor. Egg Rock Light was automated in 1976
and under the Maine Lights Program it was turned
over to the U.S. Fish and Wildlife Service; it is
within the Petit Manan National Wildlife Refuge.

(top)

Burnt Coat Harbor Light
Hockamock Head, Swan's Island

PHOTO: JEREMY D'ENTREMONT

Two range lights, with the rear light at a higher elevation, were originally constructed in 1872 at Hockamock Head to mark the entrance to Burnt Coat Harbor. Due to complaints that the two lights were confusing, the smaller front light was discontinued in 1884 and later removed. In 1994, as part of the Maine Lights Program, the Coast Guard transferred ownership of the light to the town of Swan's Island and a public park is planned for it.

(bottom)

Isle au Haut Light
Isle au Haute Thorofare, Rockport

PHOTO: © 2000 GARY P. RICHARDSON

Isle Au Haut Light with its wooden walkway was built just offshore at Robinson Point in 1907. A resident purchased the property when the light was automated in 1934. In 1986 the property, except for the lighthouse, was again sold and converted into The Keeper's House, a bed and breakfast inn. In 1998, under the Maine Lights Program, the lighthouse itself was turned over to the town of Isle Au Haut.

(top)

Perkins Island Light
Perkins Island, Kennebec River, Georgetown

PHOTO: FRANCINE DOLLINGER

Perkins Island Light was built in 1898 to assist mariners plying the waters of the Kennebec River. It was automated in 1959 and the station, except for the light, was transferred to the state of Maine. In 2000 the lighthouse was licensed to the American Lighthouse Foundation. The Friends of Perkins Island Lighthouse, a chapter of the American Lighthouse Foundation, is working for the station's restoration. It is not open to the public.

(bottom)

Petit Manan Light
Off Petit Manan Point, Milbridge

PHOTO: FRANCINE DOLLINGER

Petit Manan Light, the second tallest light in Maine, is located on Petit Manan Island, known familiarly as "tit Manan". Built in 1817, it warns of a sandbar extending beyond the island to Petit Manan Point. The present lighthouse was built in 1855. After it was automated in 1972, the island, with the exception of the light itself, was turned over to the U.S. Fish and Wildlife Service. The Coast Guard maintains the light. Today the island is a breeding colony for puffin, eiders, and terns.

(opposite)

Pemaquid Point Light
Entrance to Muscongus Bay and John Bay, Bristol

PHOTO: ANN L. HURD

Pemaquid Point Light marks the entrance to Muscongus Bay and John Bay. The original 1827 tower was replaced in 1835. In 1934, it became the first lighthouse in Maine to be automated. The 1856 fourth order Fresnel lens is still in use. In 1972 the keeper's house was converted into the Fishermen's Museum. While the town of Bristol manages the grounds, the lighthouse itself was licensed to the American Lighthouse Foundation in 2000 and continues to be maintained by them.

(top)

Matinicus Rock Light
5 miles from Matinicus Island, Penobscot Bay, Matinicus

PHOTO:© KRAIG ANDERSON

Matinicus Rock Light stands on Matinicus Rock, eighteen miles offshore on the approach to Penobscot Bay. In 1848 the two wooden towers were replaced with two granite towers. The present towers were erected in 1857 and are 180 feet apart. In 1923 the north light was decommissioned when the government decided to use single lights only. In 1998 it became the property of the U.S. Fish and Wildlife Service under the Maine Lights Program.

(bottom, left)

Goose Rocks Light
Near North Haven

PHOTO: © KRAIG ANDERSON

Goose Rocks Light was built in 1890 at the entrance to the Fox Islands Thorofare near Vinalhaven and North Haven Islands. It was automated in 1963 and is maintained by the U.S. Coast Guard.

(bottom, right)

Whitlocks Mill Light
St. Croix River, Calais

PHOTO: ROXIE ZWICKER

In 1892 Whitlocks Mill Light was established by placing a lantern in a tree on the banks of the St. Croix River. In 1910 the present lighthouse was erected establishing it as the northernmost light in the United States. Under the Maine Lights Program the property was transferred to the St. Croix Historical Society.

(top)

Whitehead Light
Whitehead Island, Penobscot Bay, St. George

PHOTO: FRANCINE DOLLINGER

Whitehead Light is located at the entrance to the Muscle Ridge Channel in West Penobscot Bay. In 1852 the original 1807 tower was replaced with the existing tower and a new keeper's house was built. In 1956 Pine Island Camp bought a portion of the island to be used as a children's camp and in 1998, under the Maine Lights Program, the station was transferred to Pine Island Camp.

(bottom)

Tenants Harbor Light
Southern Island, Tenants Harbor, St. George

PHOTO: FRANCINE DOLLINGER

Tenants Harbor Light, built in 1857, is a white cylindrical tower with an attached keeper's house on the northeast side of Southern Island. In 1934 the government decommissioned the light and sold it at auction. It was eventually purchased by artist Andrew Wyeth and his wife Betsy. Today their son, artist Jamie Wyeth, and his wife Phyllis live on the island. The bell tower replica is used as his studio.

New Hampshire

(previous page)

Portsmouth Harbor Lighthouse
Fort Constitution, Portsmouth Harbor

PHOTO: BRIAN TAGUE

In 1771 Fort William and Mary was a British military station. At that time, a wooden lighthouse was built on Great Island marking the entrance to Portsmouth Harbor. After the Revolution, the fort became known as Fort Constitution. In 1877 the present cast-iron lighthouse was built. Today the Friends of Portsmouth Harbor Lighthouse care for the lighthouse. A fourth order Fresnel lens is still in use.

(above)

White Island Light
Southern tip of White Island, Isles of Shoals

PHOTO: ROSS TRACY

The Isles of Shoals is a cluster of eighteen islands located nine miles off the shore of Portsmouth. In 1820, White Island Light was erected to guide mariners away from the shoals. In 1859 a brick tower replaced the original tower. The lighthouse was automated in 1986 and in 1993 it was turned over to the state of New Hampshire. Today, the "Lighthouse Kids" of North Hampton are working to have the lighthouse restored.

(opposite)

Loon Island Light
Lake Sunapee

PHOTO: © KRAIG ANDERSON

Loon Island Light was one of three lighthouses built in 1893 as aids to steamship navigation. It was rebuilt in 1960 after being destroyed by lighting. The lighthouse is currently owned by the state of New Hampshire and maintained by the Lake Sunapee Protective Association.

(above)

Burkehaven Light
Lake Sunapee

PHOTO: © KRAIG ANDERSON

Burkenhaven Light was one of three lighthouses built on Lake Sunapee in 1893. Around 1936 crushing ice destroyed it and the Lake Sunapee Protective Association rebuilt it in 1983. The lighthouse is currently owned by the state of New Hampshire and maintained by the Lake Sunapee Protective Association.

(opposite)

Herrick Cove Light
Lake Sunapee

PHOTO: © KRAIG ANDERSON

Herrick Cove Light was one of three lighthouses built in 1893 as an aid to steamship navigation on Lake Sunapee. It remains the only original light on the lake. It was refurbished in 1963 with additional repairs completed in 1983 and 2004. The lighthouse is currently owned by the state of New Hampshire and maintained by the Lake Sunapee Protective Association.

Vermont

(previous page)

Colchester Reef Light
Shelburne Museum (originally on Lake Champlain)

PHOTO: BRIAN BAGUE

The Colchester Reef Light was erected in 1871 to mark three dangerous shoals on Lake Champlain, about a mile into the lake from Colchester Point. In 1933 it was deactivated and fell into disrepair. The lighthouse was later sold privately and then resold to Electra Havemeyer Webb who founded the Shelburne Museum. The lighthouse was dismantled and moved to its present location where it is one of 37 buildings on the grounds of the museum.

(top and bottom)

Burlington Breakwater Lights
Burlington Harbor, Lake Champlain

PHOTO: SHIRIN PAGELS

Traffic increased after the Champlain Canal was completed in 1823, connecting Lake Champlain to the Hudson River. To protect the harbor, five granite breakwaters were built in the 1830's. Lights were then added to the north and south of the Burlington breakwater. After being automated in 1938 both lights were replaced with skeleton towers. In 2003 replica lighthouses replaced the skeleton towers.

Isle la Motte Light
Isle la Motte, Lake Champlain

PHOTO: BRIAN TAGUE

The first lighthouse that was established on the northern end of Isle la Motte was a lantern placed in a window of a house in 1829. The present lighthouse was built in 1880. In 1933 a skeleton structure replaced the light and the station was privately sold. In 2002 the Coast Guard initiated the relighting of the lighthouse and succeeded after working closely with the owners.

Juniper Island Light
Juniper Island, near Burlington

In 1826 Juniper Island Light was erected, just southwest of Burlington. The original structure was
replaced in 1846 with a 25-foot cast-iron tower,
believed to be the oldest cast-iron lighthouse in the
United States. In 1954 an automated skeleton tower
replaced the light and the island was sold privately.
The original keeper's house was destroyed in 1962 by
a fire. However, a new keeper's house was built in
2003 and work on the restoration of the tower is
planned.

Windmill Point Light
Alburg, Lake Champlain

PHOTO: © KRAIG ANDERSON

It is believed that as early as 1830 Windmill Point Light was originally a lantern hung on a post. The present lighthouse was built in 1858. In 1931 the light was replaced by a skeleton tower and sold privately. After working closely with the owners, the Coast Guard relit the lighthouse in 2002.

Massachusetts

Brant Point Light
Nantucket Island

PHOTO: WILLIAM A. BRITTEN

Brant Point Light was erected in 1746, making it America's second oldest lighthouse. Since then, it has been relocated and rebuilt more times than any other lighthouse. The present lighthouse was built in 1901. The grounds only are open to the public.

Long Point Light
Provincetown Harbor

PHOTO: ROSS TRACY

Long Point Light was built in 1826 as an aid to mariners entering Provincetown Harbor. The present lighthouse was built in 1875. The light was automated in 1952 and the keeper's house and fog signal building were destroyed. Today the lighthouse is maintained by the Cape Cod Chapter of the American Lighthouse Foundation with only the grounds open to the public.

Ten Pound Island Light
Gloucester Harbor

PHOTO: BRIAN TAGUE

Ten Pound Island Light was erected in 1821 as an aid to mariners entering Gloucester's inner harbor. In 1881 the present cast-iron lighthouse replaced the original stone structure. Ownership of the lighthouse was transferred to the city of Gloucester and in the 1980s the Lighthouse Preservation Society restored it, relighting it in 1989. Today it is an active aid to navigation.

Great Point Light
Northeast point of Nantucket Island

PHOTO: WILLIAM A. BRITTEN

A wooden tower was built on Great Point in 1784 to
mark the northeast point of Nantucket. Erosion
threatened its 1818 replacement and it was destroyed
in a 1984 storm. A replica was built in 1986, 300
yards west of the old structure. Today Great Point is
part of a wildlife refuge and is a nesting site for the
endangered piping plover. The grounds and lighthouse are open for daily tours between May and
October through the Trustees of Reservations.

Palmer's Island Light
New Bedford Harbor

PHOTO: ROSS TRACY

Palmer's Island Light was erected in 1849 on the
northern point of Palmer's Island, marking the
entrance to New Bedford Harbor. The lighthouse
was deactivated in 1963 after a hurricane wall was
constructed in New Bedford Harbor. The island
was then sold privately and over the years suffered
from neglect. In 1978 it became the property of
the city of New Bedford. In 1999, after a great
restoration effort, the lighthouse was relit.

Tarpaulin Cove Light
Naushon Island, Elizabeth Islands, Gosnold

PHOTO: BRIAN TAGUE

Prior to the erection of Tarpaulin Cove Light, tav-
ern keepers maintained a beacon for 58 years on
Naushon Island, the largest of the Elizabeth
Islands. Tarpaulin Cove Light replaced this beacon
in 1817. The original stone structure was replaced
in 1891 with the present lighthouse. Today the
Cuttyhunk Historical Society maintains the lighthouse, which is not open to the public.

Edgartown Light
Edgartown Harbor, Martha's Vineyard

PHOTO: RICK TOTTON

In 1828 Edgartown Light was built on a stone pier a short distance from the mainland. The hurricane of 1938 damaged the lighthouse and the following year it was destroyed by the Coast Guard. In 1939 the Coast Guard relocated a 1873 cast-iron tower from Crane's Beach in Ipswich to this present location. Today the Martha's Vineyard Historical Society maintains the lighthouse with only the grounds open to the public. The lighthouse also serves as a children's memorial.

(top)

Derby Wharf Light
Salem Harbor

PHOTO: BRIAN TAGUE

As Salem's fishing trade flourished, the need for an inner harbor light became apparent. In 1871 Derby Wharf Light was erected at the end of Derby Wharf. Because of its easy access, the light had caretakers rather than a resident keeper. In 1977 the light was deactivated and ownership went to the National Park Service two years later. The Friends of Salem Maritime had the light relit in 1989 and today it remains a private aid to navigation.

(bottom)

Graves Light
The Graves, Outer Boston Harbor

PHOTO: BRIAN TAGUE

In 1905 Graves Light was erected on a group of ledges called The Graves, located in Boston's outer harbor. Constructed from granite cut from Rockport, Massachusetts' quarries, Graves Light was for many years the most powerful light in New England.

(opposite)

Long Island Head Light
Long Island, Boston Harbor

PHOTO: BRIAN TAGUE

Long Island Head Light was built in 1819 as Boston's inner harbor light. Since then it has been rebuilt or moved three times. In 1844 the country's first cast-iron lighthouse replaced the original structure. The present lighthouse was built in 1901 to make room for the enlargement of Fort Strong. In 1982 it was removed from service but was relit in 1985 after being renovated by the Coast Guard. The lighthouse is not accessible to the public.

(left top)

Duxbury Pier Light
Duxbury Bay, Plymouth

Duxbury Pier Light, locally known as "The Bug", was built in 1871 to guide mariners around a dangerous shoal in Plymouth Harbor. Today Project Gurnet & Bug Lights, Inc. maintains the light.

(left, bottom)

Butler Flats Light
New Bedford Channel, New Bedford

Butler Flats Light, located in the New Bedford Channel, was erected in 1898 replacing the Clark's Point Light. It was decommissioned in 1978 and came under the control of the city of New Bedford. On its 100th birthday it was relit with a new optic and today is a private aid to navigation.

(right)

Cape Poge Light
Chappaquiddick Island, Edgartown

Cape Poge Light was built in 1802 to guide mariners into Edgartown Harbor, on Martha's Vineyard. In 1838 erosion forced the relocation of the tower back from the edge of the cliff. In 1893 a temporary wooden tower was built 40 feet inland. Since then, the tower has been moved back from the cliff three times. The grounds are open to the public, and the tower is open through tours run by the Trustees of Reservations.

Ned's Point Light
Entrance to Mattapoisett Harbor, Mattapoisett

PHOTO: BRIAN TAGUE

Ned's Point Light was built in 1838 to designate the entrance to Mattapoisett Harbor. In 1952 the lighthouse was decommissioned and the grounds were later sold to the town of Mattapoisett. The lighthouse was reactivated in 1961 and is now in a public park. The U.S. Coast Guard Auxiliary has "adopted" the lighthouse and maintains it.

West Chop Light
Tisbury, Martha's Vineyard

PHOTO: BRIAN TAGUE

West Chop Light was established in 1817 to mark
the entrance to Vineyard Haven Harbor. Over the
years erosion threatened the lighthouse and as a
result a new lighthouse was built in 1846 about
1,000 feet from the original location. The present
45-foot tower replaced this structure in 1891. A
Coast Guard family lives at the station, and a
second dwelling serves as a vacation home for
people in all branches of the military.

East Chop Light
Vineyard Haven entrance to Martha's Vineyard

PHOTO: WILLIAM A. BRITTEN

Between 1828 and 1834 a semaphore station was
located on the site of the East Chop Light. In
1869 Captain Silas Daggett privately built and
operated a lighthouse at East Chop to direct
mariners to the channel entrance of Vineyard
Haven Harbor. The government purchased land
from the captain and in 1878 East Chop Light was
established along with a keeper's house. Today the
Martha's Vineyard Historical Society cares for the
lighthouse and its surrounding grounds.

(top)

Eastern Point Light
East side of Gloucester Harbor

PHOTO: BRIAN TAGUE

In 1832 a lighthouse was built at Eastern Point, replacing an earlier day marker. The present light-house was built in 1890. Between 1894 and 1905 a 2,250-foot breakwater was built in front of the lighthouse to help shelter the harbor. Gloucester Breakwater Light sits at the end of the breakwater marking Dog Bar Reef. Today the Coast Guard retains the station for housing.

(bottom, left)

Wood End Light
Entrance to Provincetown Harbor

PHOTO: BOB MCKEON

The present 39-foot square brick Wood End Lighthouse was built in 1872 near the entrance to Provincetown Harbor. After being automated in 1961, the station was destroyed except for the tower and oil house. Today the lighthouse is main-tained by the Cape Cod Chapter of the American Lighthouse Foundation and is an active aid to navigation.

(bottom right)

Cleveland Ledge Light
Cleveland Ledge Channel, Bourne

PHOTO: BRIAN TAGUE

Cleveland Ledge Light, built in 1943, was the last commissioned lighthouse built in New England. Its unique style is classified as Art Moderne. It is the only lighthouse built by the Coast Guard after they took control of the nation's lighthouses in 1939.

Boston Light
Little Brewster Island, Boston Harbor

PHOTO: BRIAN TAGUE

Boston Light, America's first light station, was lit in 1716. In 1776 the British destroyed it and it was rebuilt in 1783. In 1859 it was raised 14 feet to a height of 89 feet. The beacon was extinguished during World War II and relit in 1945 with an 1859 second order Fresnel lens. In 2003 a civilian keeper, America's only official lighthouse keeper, was appointed. The Coast Guard Auxiliary also works on the island. Tours are available in the summer through mid-October.

Chatham Light
Chatham Harbor

PHOTO: BRIAN TAGUE

Chatham Light, located in Chatham Harbor, was built in 1808 as a twin light station, differentiating it from Highland Light. Twin octagonal wood towers were built about 70 feet apart with a small one-room keeper's house. In 1923 the north light was moved to Nauset Beach to become Nauset Light while the southern light remained. The duplex dwellings serves as U.S. Coast Guard Station Chatham.

Baker's Island Light
Baker's Island, approach to Salem Harbor

PHOTO: BRIAN TAGUE

Baker's Island Light was originally established in 1791 as a day marker. In 1798 twin towers were built atop the keeper's house, about 40 feet apart. After one light was extinguished in 1816, new towers were built in 1820. They were known as the Mr. and Mrs. Lighthouses, as one was taller. In 1926 the smaller lighthouse was demolished. Today the keeper's house is leased out in the summer and the Baker's Island Association manages the island.

(top)

Monomoy Point Light
South Monomoy Island, Chatham

PHOTO: BRIAN TAGUE

Monomoy Point Light was built in 1823 to warn
mariners of dangerous shoals. The original wooden
tower and keeper's house were replaced in 1849 with
the present cast-iron structure. The lighthouse was
deactivated in 1923 and was sold into private hands
after the Chatham Light received a more powerful
optic. The blizzard of 1978 divided the peninsula
into two islands, north and south. Today Monomoy
National Wildlife Refuge maintains the lighthouse.

(bottom, left and right)

Nauset Light and Three Sisters
Nauset Light Beach, Eastham

NAUSET LIGHT PHOTO (L): RICHARD ASARISI
THREE SISTERS PHOTO (R): WILLIAM A. BRITTEN

A light station was established on Nauset Beach in
1838. To differentiate this station from Highland
Light and the twin lights of Chatham, three identi-
cal "sister" lighthouses were built. In 1911 the
center lighthouse was moved back due to erosion
and the two remaining lighthouses were privately
sold and moved to Cable Road, about 1,800 feet
from Nauset Light. The present lighthouse was

replaced in 1923 with the twin north light from
Chatham. The three sisters were reunited in 1975
when the National Park Service purchased the relocated towers and placed them in their original con-
figuration on Cable Road. Today Nauset Light is a
private aid to navigation and is managed by the
Nauset Light Preservation Society.

Scituate Light
Cedar Point, Scituate

PHOTO: JEREMY D'ENTREMONT

Scituate Light was built in 1811 to aid mariners entering the shallow waters of Scituate Harbor. The lighthouse was decommissioned in 1850 when Minot's Ledge Light was completed. The property was transferred to the town of Scituate in 1916 and later in 1968 the Scituate Historical Society was awarded custody and administration of the lighthouse. The lighthouse was relit in 1994 and today is a private aid to navigation.

Hospital Point Light
Hospital Point, Beverly

PHOTO: JEREMY D'ENTREMONT

Hospital Point Light was built in 1872 to guide mariners into Salem and Beverly harbors. The two-story brick keeper's house was built in the Federal design and has had two major additions. It became a range light in 1927 when a light was placed in the steeple of Beverly's First Baptist Church. Today both lights remain active aids to navigation. The keeper's house became the residence of the Commander of the First Coast Guard District in the 1940's.

Borden Flats Light
Taunton River, Fall River

PHOTO: BRIAN TAGUE

In 1881 Borden Flats Light was erected on a reef at the mouth of the Taunton River in Fall River. The location was named after the family of the infamous Lizzie Borden and today remains an active aid to navigation.

Sandy Neck Light
Entrance to Barnstable Harbor, Barnstable

PHOTO: BRIAN TAGUE

Sandy Neck Light was built in 1826 on a seven-mile peninsula on the west side of the entrance to Barnstable Harbor. In 1857 the original structure was replaced with the present lighthouse. The two iron hoops located on the tower were installed in 1887 to strengthen the brick tower. In 1931 the lighthouse was decommissioned and replaced by a skeleton tower. Today the lighthouse is privately owned.

Thacher Island Twin Lights
Thacher Island, off Cape Ann, Rockport

PHOTO: BRIAN TAGUE

Thacher Island Twin Lights, originally built in 1771, is today the only operating twin light station in America. The present 124-foot-tall towers replaced the originals in 1861. The south light was automated in 1980 and the north light, decommissioned in 1932, was relit in 1989. The town of Rockport and the Thacher Island Association maintain the island while the Coast Guard maintains the south light. Camping and overnight accommodations are offered during the summer.

Sankaty Head Light
Siasconset, Nantucket Island

PHOTO: WILLIAM A. BRITTEN

Sankaty Head Light, built in 1850 on the southeastern elbow of Nantucket Island, was the first lighthouse in the United States to have a Fresnel lens as part of its original equipment. Over the years, erosion has threatened the station and as a result the keeper's house and remaining buildings were removed from the site. Erosion control measures have been taken but it will only be a matter of time before the lighthouse itself will need to be moved away from the bluff.

Annisquam Light
Wigwam Point, Gloucester

PHOTO: ROSS TRACY

In 1801 the first lighthouse tower and keeper's house were erected on Wigwam Point in Annisquam to prevent groundings on Squam Bar. A new octagonal tower was built in 1851. This tower was replaced in 1897 with the present 41-foot brick lighthouse. Today it houses a Coast Guard family.

(left and right)

Newburyport Range Lights
Newburyport Harbor

PHOTOS: BRIAN TAGUE *(left)*
JEREMY D'ENTREMONT *(right)*

The Newburyport Range Lights were erected in 1873 as an aid to mariners entering Newburyport Harbor and to mark Goose Rocks. The front light was erected on Bayley's Wharf, while the rear pyramidal light was erected on what is now Water Street. The lights were discontinued in 1961 and the rear light was privately sold. The front light was moved to its present location in 1964 and today is part of the Coast Guard Station Merrimack River.

Plum Island Light
Northern tip of Plum Island, Newburyport

PHOTO: BRIAN TAGUE

Twin wooden range lighthouses, built on movable foundations, were the first to be erected on the northern tip of Plum Island. The continuously shifting sandbar around Plum Island necessitated the adjustment of the lighthouses in order to direct mariners into Newburyport Harbor. The existing tower was erected in 1898. In 2003 the lighthouse was transferred to the city of Newburyport and it is managed by the Friends of Plum Island Light, Inc. Occasionally it is open to the public.

(left)

Straitsmouth Island Light
Rockport

PHOTO: JEREMY D'ENTREMONT

Straitsmouth Island Light was built in 1835 to aid mariners into Pigeon Cove and through the channel between Thacher Island and the Salvages. The present lighthouse was built in 1896. In 1941 the island, except for the lighthouse, was sold privately. It was donated to the Massachusetts Audubon Society in the 1960's. The light remains an active aid to navigation.

(right)

Wing's Neck Light
Pocasset, east side of Buzzards Bay, Bourne

PHOTO: BRIAN TAGUE

Wing's Neck Light was built in 1848 to guide mariners around the peninsula into Buzzards Bay. The present lighthouse was built in 1890. In 1923 the keeper's house from Ned Point Light was floated on a barge across Buzzards Bay to its present location to serve as the assistant keeper's house. Wing's Neck Light was decommissioned after the Cleveland Ledge Light was established. Today the lighthouse is privately owned and is available as a vacation rental.

Point Gammon Light
Great Island, entrance to Hyannis Harbor, Barnstable

PHOTO: BRIAN TAGUE

Point Gammon Light was erected on Great Island
in 1816 to aid mariners navigating the area. The
lighthouse was discontinued in 1858 when a lightship was anchored near Bishops and Clerks ledges.
It was later sold and has remained privately owned.

(top)

Race Point Light
Northern tip of Cape Cod, Provincetown

PHOTO: FREDERICK A. MEDINA

Built near the northernmost tip of Cape Cod, Race Point Light signals mariners around the sandbars near Race Point. In 1876 a cast-iron lighthouse replaced the original stone tower. In 1995 the property was leased to the American Lighthouse Foundation and has since undergone a complete restoration. Today the property is used as a research facility and also offers overnight accommodations.

(bottom, left)

Fort Pickering Light
Winter Island, Salem Harbor, Salem

PHOTO: ROSS TRACY

Fort Pickering Light was built on Winter Island in 1871 to guide mariners into Salem Harbor. Fort Pickering was used during the War of 1812, the Spanish American War and the Civil War. The lighthouse was deactivated in 1969 and replaced by an offshore buoy. The blizzard of '78 tore its door off and it remained in the harbor until the Fort Pickering Light Association retrieved it for refurbishment. It was relit in 1983 and is a private aid to navigation.

(bottom, right)

Hyannis Harbor Light
Hyannis Harbor, Cape Cod, Barnstable

PHOTO: © KRAIG ANDERSON

Hyannis Harbor Light was built in 1849 to replace a privately built and maintained structure. A range light was added in 1885 on the Old Colony Railroad Wharf. The Hyannis Harbor Light was decommissioned in 1929 and sold at auction. The lighthouse remains privately owned.

Nobska Light
Woods Hole Harbor entrance, Woods Hole

PHOTO: PAULA DUNBAR

Nobska Light was established in 1829 to guide vessels into Woods Hole Harbor. The present lighthouse was built in 1876. The Coast Guard took over management of the lighthouse in 1939 and today it is housing for the Commander of the U.S. Coast Guard Group Woods Hole. An 1888 fourth order Fresnel lens is still in use today. The lighthouse is occasionally open to the public.

(top)

Gay Head Light
Gay Head Cliffs, Martha's Vineyard

Gay Head Light, located on the western shore of Martha's Vineyard, sits atop a spectacular 130-foot multicolored cliff. It was first lit in 1799 to aid mariners navigating Vineyard Sound from Buzzards Bay. The present lighthouse was built in 1856. It is maintained by The Martha's Vineyard Historical Society and is open to the public from mid-June to August, one hour before sunset to ½ hour after sunset.

(bottom, left)

Marblehead Light
Marblehead Neck, approach to Salem and Marblehead Harbors

Marblehead Light was originally a 20-foot-tall white brick tower with an attached keeper's house. When new houses eventually obscured its light, a light was attached to the top of a 100-foot mast and remained there from 1883 to 1895. This makeshift light was replaced in 1896 with the present brown skeleton tower. Today the lighthouse is licensed to the town of Marblehead.

(bottom, right)

Minot's Ledge Light
Cohasset Rocks, south of Boston Harbor

The first lighthouse built on Cohasset Rocks in 1850 was a 70-foot-high "iron pile" structure that stood upon nine legs. Atop was the keeper's quarters and lantern room. This structure lasted until 1851 when a storm swept it away killing two keepers. The present lighthouse, completed in 1860, has been called "the greatest achievement in American lighthouse engineering." Before being automated in 1947, it was considered one of the most dangerous posts due to the huge waves that would break over the 114-foot tall structure.

Bass River Light
West Dennis

PHOTO: © KRAIG ANDERSON

In 1855 the Bass River Light was established to aid mariners navigating the Bass River entrance. It was decommissioned in 1880 and sold after the Stage Harbor Light in Chatham was lit. It was relit in 1881 after numerous complaints and was removed from service permanently in 1914 when the Cape Cod Canal opened. In 1938 Senator Everett Stone purchased the light. Soon after, it was opened as the Lighthouse Inn and in 1989 the beacon was relit. Today it is recognized as the West Dennis Light.

Stage Harbor Light
Harding's Beach, Chatham

PHOTO: FREDERICK A. MEDINA

Stage Harbor Light, located on Harding's Beach, was built in 1880 to guide mariners into Stage Harbor. In 1933 a skeleton tower replaced the light and the tower was capped. It was privately sold and today remains a private residence.

Bird Island Light
Sippican Harbor, Marion

PHOTO: © KRAIG ANDERSON

Bird Island Light was built in 1819 off Butlers Point in Marion and remained the only lighthouse in Buzzards Bay until 1837 when Ned's Point was constructed. In 1933 it was decommissioned and the island was sold to a private party in 1940. The hurricane of 1938 destroyed every building on Bird Island except the lighthouse tower. In 1966 it became the property of the town of Marion and today the Bird Island Light Preservation Society maintains it. In 1997 it was relit as a private aid to navigation.

Highland Light (Cape Cod Light)
North Truro

PHOTO: PAULA DUNBAR

Highland Light was built in 1797 on the east side of Cape Cod to warn mariners of the Peaked Hill Bars. The present lighthouse was built in 1857. Erosion threatened the lighthouse and in 1996 it was relocated 450 feet back from the cliff. Today the Highland Museum and Lighthouse, Inc. cares for the lighthouse with the lighthouse open for tours from May to October.

Rhode Island

(previous page)

Castle Hill Light
East passage of Narragansett Bay, Newport

PHOTO: WILLIAM A. BRITTEN

Castle Hill Lighthouse was built in 1890 to aid navigation of the east passage of the Narragansett Bay. It continues to be an active aid to navigation.

(top)

Poplar Point Light
Wickford Harbor, Wickford

PHOTO: BURT GUERIN

Poplar Point Light, a keeper's dwelling with a wooden tower attached to the roof, was built in 1831 to mark the entrance of Wickford Harbor. In 1882 the light was replaced by Wickford Harbor Light and sold privately. It remains privately owned.

(bottom)

Rose Island Light
North of Newport Harbor, Newport

PHOTO: BOB MCKEON

Rose Island Light was built in 1870 on the southwest corner of Rose Island to aid mariners through the east passage of Narragansett Bay. After the Newport Bridge was complete in 1969, the Coast Guard decommissioned it in 1971. Over time it fell into disrepair. The Rose Island Lighthouse Foundation, formed in 1985, restored it to its 1912–1915 period. It was relit in 1993 and today it is a living history museum and environmental education center. Overnight stays are available.

Prudence Island Light
Narragansett Bay, Portsmouth

PHOTO: BRIAN TAGUE

In 1851 Goat Island's former 1823 lighthouse tower was moved to Prudence Island and a keeper's house was built, thus establishing Prudence Island Light. Prudence Island Light marks the dangerous passage between Prudence Island and the mainland. The lighthouse is now licensed to a group called the Prudence Conservancy with only the grounds open to the public.

(above)

Point Judith Light
West side of entrance to Narragansett Bay,
Narragansett

PHOTO: ROSS TRACY

Point Judith Light was erected in 1810 to guide
mariners to the entrance of Narragansett Bay. The
present lighthouse was built in 1857 and the
fourth order Fresnel lens is still in use today.
The grounds only are open to the public.

(opposite)

Beavertail Light
Conanicut Island, Jamestown

PHOTO: FRANCINE DOLLINGER

Beavertail Light is located on the southern tip of
Conanicut Island at the entrance to Narragansett
Bay. The original wooden tower was built in 1749
and was the third lighthouse erected in the United
States. The present tower was built in 1856. In
1898 an assistant keeper's house was built, which
today houses the Beavertail Lighthouse Museum.

(top)

Newport Harbor Light
Newport Harbor, Newport

PHOTO: RICK TOTTON

Newport Harbor Light was erected on the northern tip of Goat Island in 1823. In 1842 a breakwater was built and a new lighthouse was erected.
The original lighthouse was moved to Prudence
Island where it remains today. The present lighthouse was built in 1842 and today is on the
grounds of the Hyatt Regency. The American
Lighthouse Foundation maintains it.

(bottom)

Watch Hill Light
Fishers Island Sound east approach, Westerly

PHOTO: RICK TOTTON

Watch Hill Light, Rhode Island's second lighthouse, was built in 1807. It was the original location of the watchtower during King George's War
in the 1740's. Due to the threat of erosion, the
present tower and keeper's house were built farther
back in 1856. After being automated in 1986, the
lighthouse was leased to the Watch Hill Light
Keepers Association. Today there is a small museum in the oil house.

Nayatt Point Light
Nayatt Point, Barrington

PHOTO: © 2000 ANNA P. KLEIN

Nayatt Point Light was built in 1828 to guide mariners past the shoal off Conimicut Point. The present lighthouse was built in 1856. In 1868 the Conimicut Point Light was built, which made Nayatt Point Light unnecessary. It was discontinued at that time and sold privately.

(top)

Pomham Rocks Light
East side of the Providence River, Providence

Pomham Rocks Light, located in the Providence River, was erected in 1871. In 1974 the lighthouse was decommissioned and replaced by a skeleton tower. In 1980 the Mobil Oil Company, with a refinery and terminal nearby, purchased the property and continues to maintain it.

(bottom)

Lime Rock Light
Newport Harbor, Newport

Lime Rock Light in Newport Harbor was first built in 1854 with a keeper's house added in 1856. In 1857 keeper Hosea Lewis had a stroke and left the lighthouse duties to his daughter, Ida. She remained keeper until her death in 1911. During her tenure she rescued many and is one of the most celebrated lighthouse keepers in American history. The lighthouse was discontinued in 1927 and later sold, becoming the Ida Lewis Yacht Club.

(opposite)

Conanicut Island Light
North end of Conanicut Island, Jamestown

Conanicut Lighthouse was built in 1886 to aid mariner's navigating this dangerous point. It was deactivated in 1933 and sold privately.

(top, left)

Plum Beach Light
Near north Kingston

PHOTO: JEREMY D'ENTREMONT

Plum Beach Light was built in 1899 to aid mariners through the west passage of Narragansett Bay. In 1941 the Jamestown Bridge was completed making Plum Beach Light obsolete. It fell into disrepair until 1999 when it was transferred to the Friends of Plum Beach Lighthouse. The exterior has been restored and the light relit as a private aid to navigation.

(top, right)

Block Island North Light
Sandy Point, north end of Block Island

PHOTO: RICK TOTTON

Block Island North Light was originally two lights on either end of a building, marking the entrance to Block Island and Long Island Sounds. The present lighthouse was built in 1867. In 1973 it was deactivated and taken over by the United States Fish and Wildlife Service. A skeleton tower was placed a short distance away. In 1984 it was sold to the town of New Shoreham and was renovated and relit in 1989 with the first floor opened as a museum.

(bottom)

Warwick Light
Warwick Neck, Warwick

PHOTO: FRANCINE DOLLINGER

Warwick Light was first built on Warwick Neck in 1826 to aid mariners passing between Patience Island and the Neck. The present lighthouse was built in 1932. After the hurricane of 1938 there was so much erosion that the lighthouse was moved back 50 feet in order to avoid sliding over the cliff. Today the keeper's house is used for Coast Guard housing.

Block Island Southeast Light
Mohegan Bluffs, Block Island

PHOTO: FRANCINE DOLLINGER

Built in 1875 about 300 feet from the bluff, the
Block Island Southeast Light is a unique Gothic
Revival architectural showcase. In 1990 it was deactivated and replaced with a skeleton structure. After
raising two million dollars, the Block Island Southeast Lighthouse Foundation had the lighthouse
moved back 300 feet as erosion had taken some 250
feet of the bluff. There is a museum and gift shop in
the lighthouse and tours are offered in the summer.

(above)

Hog Island Shoal Light
East passage of Narragansett Bay, near Portsmouth

PHOTO: JEREMY D'ENTREMONT

The first beacon to warn mariners of the dangerous shoals near Hog Island was a lightship. In 1901 the present conical cast iron tower replaced the lightship. It remains an active aid to navigation.

(opposite)

Bristol Ferry Light
Bristol

PHOTO: © KRAIG ANDERSON

The Bristol Ferry Lighthouse was built in 1855 to aid in the navigation of the narrow passage between Mount Hope Bay and Narragansett Bay. In 1927 it was decommissioned and replaced by a skeleton tower. The government sold the property in 1928 and it has remained privately owned since.

Conimicut Shoal Light
Conimicut Point, near Barrington

PHOTO: JEREMY D'ENTREMONT

Conimicut Shoal Light is located on a dangerous shoal in the Providence River, between Conimicut Point and Nayatt Point. The original granite tower was built in 1868 and keepers had to row one mile to tend to it. In 1883 the old tower was torn down and the present sparkplug-style lighthouse with living quarters was erected. It remains an active aid to navigation.

Dutch Island Light
West passage of Narragansett Bay, near Jamestown

PHOTO: JEREMY D'ENTREMONT

In 1826 Dutch Island Light was built to mark the west passage of Narragansett Bay. The present lighthouse was built in 1857. During the Civil War and World War I the island served as an encampment. The island was later deeded to the state of Rhode Island for the conservation of wildlife. In 1979 the lighthouse was discontinued and replaced by offshore buoys. In 2000, the Dutch Island Lighthouse Society, a chapter of the American Lighthouse Foundation, was formed and restoration is planned.

Sakonnet Point Light
Little Cormorant Rock, Little Compton

Sakonnet Point Light was built in 1884 on Little Cormorant Rock at the mouth of the Sakonnet River. After being damaged in the hurricanes of 1938 and 1954, the Coast Guard decommissioned the light and sold it at auction in 1961. It was donated in 1985 to the Friends of Sakonnet Point Lighthouse, Inc. and it was restored and relit in 1997.

Connecticut

(previous page)

Mystic Seaport Light
Mystic

PHOTO: WILLIAM A. BRITTEN

Mystic Seaport —The Museum of America and the Sea—is the nation's leading maritime museum. Its lighthouse on the banks of the historic Mystic River is a replica of Brant Point Lighthouse in Nantucket. Like the Brant Point Lighthouse, it contains a fourth order Fresnel lens. Mystic Seaport was founded in 1929 and continues to tell stories of America and the sea that connects us all.

(above)

Faulkner's Island Light
Long Island Sound, Guilford

PHOTO © RICHARD ASARISI

Faulkner's Island Light, located about three miles south of Guilford, was constructed in 1802 to aid vessels navigating through Long Island Sound. The lighthouse now sits only 35 feet from the bluff due to progressive erosion. The Faulkner's Light Brigade was formed to preserve the light and the U.S. Army Corps have implemented erosion control methods.

(opposite)

Stratford Point Light
Mouth of the Housatonic River, Stratford

PHOTO: BRIAN TAGUE

Stratford Point Light was built in 1822 to mark the mouth of the Housatonic River. In 1881 a new tower was erected and the original keeper's house was replaced with the current Gothic Revival house. Today a Coast Guard family lives in the keeper's house.

(above)

Stratford Shoal Light
Western Long Island Sound, Bridgeport

PHOTO: JEREMY D'ENTREMONT

Stratford Shoal Light, built in 1877, is an octagonal granite tower with an attached dwelling located on a reef in Long Island Sound. It remains an active aid to navigation.

(opposite)

Avery Point Light
Avery Point, Groton

PHOTO: FRANCINE DOLLINGER

In 1942 the Coast Guard built the Avery Point Light and established the Groton Training Station. The light is located on the University of Connecticut's Avery Point campus and was the last built in Connecticut. After being deactivated in 1967 the property reverted back to the state. In 1999 the American Lighthouse Foundation began raising money for restoration. Soon afterward the Avery Point Lighthouse Society was created. Restoration work has begun on the lighthouse.

(above)

Morgan Point Light
West side of the mouth of the Mystic River, Noank

PHOTO: BRIAN TAGUE

Morgan Point Light was erected in 1831 to assist mariners entering the Mystic River. The original structure was a 25-foot granite tower with a separate keeper's house. That lighthouse was replaced in 1868 with the present granite structure and attached light tower. In 1919 the lighthouse was decommissioned when an automatic beacon was placed at the channel entrance to Mystic River. The lighthouse was sold to a private party.

(opposite)

Sheffield Island Light
Sheffield Islands, Norwalk

PHOTO: FRANCINE DOLLINGER

Sheffield Island Light was built in 1828, marking the ledges at the entrance to Norwalk Harbor. The present limestone-block keeper's house with attached tower was built in 1868. In 1902 Greens Ledge Light was built and replaced Sheffield Island Light, which was then sold. In 1986 the Norwalk Seaport Association purchased the island and lighthouse and maintains it as a museum and nature preserve. Public tours are offered throughout the summer.

(top)

Latimer Reef Light
Fishers Island Sound

PHOTO: RICK TOTTON

Latimer Reef Light, one mile from Fishers Island Sound, was built in 1884 to mark the western end of Latimer Reef. A buoy marks the reef's eastern end. The light remains an active aid to navigation.

(bottom)

New London Harbor Light
West side of the entrance to New London Harbor

PHOTO: RICK TOTTON

The original New London Harbor Light, built in 1761, was the first Connecticut lighthouse and the fourth lighthouse built in the United States. That structure was replaced in 1801 by the present lighthouse. The light was automated in 1912 and the property sold at auction to a private party. The lighthouse remains an active aid to navigation and continues to use an 1857 fourth order Fresnel lens.

Penfield Reef Light
Long Island Sound, near Farifield

PHOTO: © KRAIG ANDERSON

Penfield Reef Light was built in 1874 on Penfield Reef, a one-mile long rock formation. The lighthouse was automated in 1971 and remains an active aid to navigation.

(top)

Southwest Ledge Light
near New Haven

Southwest Ledge Light was built in 1877 on a dangerous rock formation about one mile from New Haven Harbor, replacing Five Mile Point Lighthouse. It remains an active aid to navigation.

(bottom)

Stamford Harbor Light
Stamford Harbor, Stamford

Stamford Harbor Light was built on Chatham Ledge in 1882 to mark the entrance to Stamford Harbor. In 1953 the lighthouse was decommissioned and it was sold in 1955. Renovated in the 1980's, it remains privately owned and is lit as a private aid to navigation.

(opposite)

Lynde Point Light
Mouth of the Connecticut River, Old Saybrook

Lynde Point Light was constructed in 1803 to mark the entrance to the Connecticut River. The present 65-foot tower was built in 1838 after the original proved too short. Today an 1890 fifth order Fresnel lens is still in use while the keeper's house is used for Coast Guard housing.

Stonington Harbor Light
East side of Stonington Harbor, Stonington

PHOTO: © KRAIG ANDERSON

Stonington Harbor Light was built in 1823 on
Windmill Point, located on the west side of
Stonington Harbor, to mark the entrance to the
harbor. The present lighthouse was built in 1840.
In 1889 a lighthouse was erected on the breakwater
in Stonington Harbor, causing Stonington Harbor
Light to be discontinued. The Stonington
Historical Society acquired the property in 1925
and it was converted into a museum.

Great Captain Island Light
Western Long Island Sound, Greenwich

PHOTO: © KRAIG ANDERSON

Great Captain Island Light, erected in 1829, is one
of three lighthouses marking the entrance to New
York City's East River. The present lighthouse was
built in 1868. The lighthouse was replaced in 1970
by a skeleton structure and the lighthouse was later
acquired by the town of Greenwich. In 1998 the
Greenwich Chamber of Commerce began a
fundraising campaign and hopes to relight the
lighthouse in the near future.

(left)

Greens Ledge Light
Norwalk Islands, Norwalk

PHOTO: © KRAIG ANDERSON

Greens Ledge Light, built in 1902, marks a one-mile ledge off the entrance to Norwalk Harbor. The light was automated in 1972 and is an active aid to navigation.

(right)

Pecks Ledge Light
Norwalk Islands, Norwalk

PHOTO: © KRAIG ANDERSON

Pecks Ledge Light was built in 1906 to mark Pecks Ledge at the east end of the Norwalk Islands on Long Island Sound. It was automated in 1933 and is an active aid to navigation.

(opposite)

Fayerweather Island Light
Fayerweather Island, Bridgeport

PHOTO: PAULA DUNBAR

Fayerweather Island Light was built in 1808 to guide mariners into Black Rock Harbor. An 1821 hurricane destroyed the tower and the present tower was built in 1823. After being deactivated in 1932, the lighthouse was turned over to the city of Bridgeport to become part of Seaside Park. The lighthouse was restored in 1998.

(above)

Saybrook Breakwater Light
Mouth of the Connecticut River

PHOTO:© KRAIG ANDERSON

In the 1870's the channel at the entrance to the Connecticut River was deepened and two breakwaters were built. The Saybrook Breakwater Light, also known as the Outer Light, was erected in 1886 on the west jetty. It was automated in 1959 and continues to be an active aid to navigation.

(opposite)

New London Ledge Light
Thames River, entrance to New London Harbor

PHOTO : © KRAIG ANDERSON

The New London Ledge Light was built in 1909 on a ledge one mile from the east entrance to New London Harbor. This one-of-a-kind lighthouse was built to appease the wealthy homeowners along the shore who wanted an edifice harmonious with the stateliness of their own homes. Today the lighthouse is leased to the New London Ledge Lighthouse Foundation. They hope to convert the structure into a museum and bed and breakfast.

(above)

Tongue Point Light
West side of Bridgeport Harbor, Bridgeport

PHOTO: FRANCINE DOLLINGER

In 1894 a small light was placed at the end of a breakwater, marking the entrance to Bridgeport Harbor. That light was replaced the following year with the Tongue Point Light, also known as Bridgeport Breakwater Light. After the shipping channel was widened in 1920, the light was moved closer to shore by 275 feet. Today the lighthouse remains an active aid to navigation.

(opposite)

Five Mile Point Light
New Haven Harbor, New Haven

PHOTO: © KRAIG ANDERSON

Five Mile Point Light, named after its distance from downtown New Haven, was built in 1805 to mark the entrance to New Haven Harbor. In 1847 the lighthouse was replaced with the present structure. It became obsolete in 1877 when Southwest Ledge Light was built. In 1922 the lighthouse became the property of the city of New Haven and today is part of the Lighthouse Point Park. The lighthouse is open for limited tours.

PHOTOGRAHPHERS

Kraig Anderson
www.lighthousefriends.com
kraig@lighthousefriends.com
*pages 8, 17, 24(2), 26, 42(2), 47, 48, 49, 55,
82, 85, 86, 97, 101, 103, 113, 116, 117, 118(2),
120, 121, 123*

Richard Asarisi
135 Oberlin Road
Hamden, CT 06514
www.photoworkings.com
pages 12, 14, 15, 27, 29, 34, 35, 72, 106

William A. Britten
1917 Stonehills Place
Knoxville, TN 37938
www.lighthousegetaway.com
*pages fronticepiece, 2–3, 6–7, 19, 20, 23, 25, 34,
56–57, 59, 67, 72, 76, 88–89, 104–105, back jacket*

Bill Collette
American Lighthouse Foundation
90 Suomi Road
Hyannis, MA 02601
page 38

Robert A. Dennis
18 Orchard Crossing
Andover, MA 01810
"Images of New England"
www.portimages.com
RAD1212@aol.com
page 13

Jeremy D'Entremont
125 Bluefish Blvd.
Portsmouth, NH 03801
www.lighthouse.cc
*pages 20, 22, 26, 28, 34, 35, 39, 64, 74(2),
78, 80, 96(2), 98, 100, 102(2), 108*

Francine Dollinger
3 Darien Court
Old Bridge, NJ 08857
*pages 12, 38, 40(2), 43(2), 84, 93, 98, 99,
109, 111, 122*

Paula Dunbar
16B Cronin Hill Road
Hatfield, MA 01038
www.croninhillphotography.com
paula@croninhillphotography.com
pages 83, 87, 119

Bert Guerin
39 Elvira Street
Bellingham, MA 02019
pages 11, 16, 28, 36, 90

Ann L. Hurd
7325 Calle de Fuente
Carlsbad, CA 92009
ann@peoplepc.com
page 41

Anna P. Klein
17 Nashoba Drive
Boxborough, MA 01719
www.cyberlights.com
pages 16, 33, 95

Chris Ledwith USCG
cledwith@gruportme.uscg.mil
page 54

The Lighthouse People
Bob & Sandra Shanklin
517 Thornhill Road
Ft. Walton Beach, FL 32547
www.thelighthousepeople.com
pages 12, 22, 30(3), 31, 32(2)

Bob McKeon
19 George Street
N. Attleboro, MA 02760
pages 68, 73, 90

Frederick A. Medina
4 East Street
Bridgewater, MA 02324
famedina@earthlink.net
pages 82, 84, 86

Shirin Pagels
9 Pulaski Street
Apt. 3G
Norwalk, CT 06851
New England Lighthouse Lovers
www.nell.cc
pages 52(2), 84, 114

Gary P. Richardson
17 Nashoba Drive
Boxborough, MA 01719
www.cyberlights.com
pages 10, 26, 37, 39

Marilyn Stiborek
www.lighthousefriends.com
marilyn_stiborek@yahoo.com
pages 28, 114

Brian Tague
82 Elm Street
Stoneham, MA 02180
www.briantague.com
*pages front jacket, 4–5, 8, 9, 18, 44–45, 50–51, 53,
58, 60, 62(2), 63, 64, 65, 66, 68(2), 69, 70, 71, 72,
73, 74, 75, 76, 78, 79, 80, 81, 91, 107, 110, 115,
back jacket*

Scott R. Thorp
7 Cider Hill Road
Rochester, NH 03867
www.themaineimage.com
pages 21, 32, 37(2)

Rick Totton
719 Still Hill Road
Hamden, CT 06518
www.rickslighthouses.com
pages 16, 61, 94(2), 98, 112(2)

Ross Tracy
www.lightdreamer.com
pages 36(2), 46, 58, 60, 64, 77, 82, 92, back jacket

Roxie Zwicker
39 Boush Street
Kittery, ME 03904
www.roxiez.com
page 42

American Lighthouse Foundation
P.O. Box 889
Wells, Maine 04090
www.lighthousefoundation.org

Avery Point Lighthouse Society
P.O. Box 1552
Groton, CT 06340
www.apls.tripod.com

Beavertail Lighthouse Museum Association
P.O. Box 83
Jamestown, RI 02835
www.beavertaillight.org

Bird Island Light Preservation Society
2 Spring Street
Marion, MA 02738
www.by-the-sea.com/birdislandlight

Block Island North Light Association
P. O. Box 1662
Block Island, RI 02807

Block Island Southeast Lighthouse Foundation
P.O. Box 949
Block Island, RI 02807

Cobbosseecontee Yacht Club
P.O. Box 17
Manchester, ME 04351

College of the Atlantic
105 Eden St.
Bar Harbor, ME 04609
www.coa.edu

Cuttyhunk Historical Society
3 Broadway
Cuttyhunk, MA 02713

Dutch Island Lighthouse Society
P.O. Box 435
Saunderstown, RI 02874
www.dutchislandlighthouse.org

Eagle Light Caretakers
c/o Sam Howe
2742 Normandy Drive NW
Atlanta, GA 30305

Faulkner's Light Brigade
P.O. Box 199
Guilford, Connecticut 06437
www.lighthouse.cc/FLB/

Fayerweather Island Restoration Fund
c/o Burroughs Community Center
2470 Fairfield Avenue
Bridgeport, CT 06605

The Fishermen's Museum
Pemaquid Point Road
New Harbor, Maine 04554

Friends of Doubling Point Light
c/o Betsy Skillings-Colemen
HCR 33 BOX 61B
Arrowsic, ME 04530
www.doublingpoint.org

Friends of Little River Light, c/o American
Lighthouse Foundation
P.O. Box 889
Wells, Maine 04090

Friends of Nash Island Light
P.O. Box 250
Addison, Maine 04606

Friends of Nubble Light
186 York Street
York, ME 03909
www.yorknet.org/ykpkrec/friends.htm

Friends of Pemaquid Point Lighthouse
c/o Richard Melville
P.O. Box 125
Bristol, ME 04539

Friends of Perkins Island Lighthouse
c/o Dr. Jane Beaulieu
P.O. Box 376
Georgetown, ME 04548

Friends of Plum Beach Lighthouse, Inc
P.O. Box 1041
North Kingstown, RI 02852
www.plumbeachlighthouse.org

The Friends of Plum Island Light, Inc
P.O. Box 381
Newburyport, MA 01950

Friends of Portsmouth Harbor Lighthouse
P.O. Box 5092
Portsmouth, NH 03802-5092
www.portsmouthharborlighthouse.org

Friends of Rockland Breakwater Lighthouse
P.O. Box 741
Rockland, ME 04841
www.rocklandlighthouse.com

The Friends of Sakonnet Point Lighthouse, Inc
P.O. Box 154
Little Compton, RI 02837

Friends of Sequin Island Light, Inc
P.O. Box 866
Bath, ME 04530
www.seguinisland.org

Friends of Wood Island Lighthouse
P. O. Box 26
Biddeford Pool, ME 04006
www.woodislandlighthouse.org

Highland Museum and Lighthouse, Inc.
P.O. Box 486
Truro, MA 02666
www.trurohistorical.org

Ida Lewis Yacht Club
P.O. Box 479
Newport, RI 02840
www.ilyc.org

Island Heritage Trust
P.O. Box 42
Deer Isle, ME 04627
www.mltn.org

Island Institute
P.O. Box 648
386 Main Street
Rockland, ME 04841
www.islandinstitute.org

The Keeper's House
P.O. Box 26
Isle Au Haut, ME 04645
www.keepershouse.com

Kennebunkport Conservation Trust
P.O. Box 7028
Cape Porpoise, ME 04014
www.thekennebunkportconservationtrust.org

Lake Sunapee Protective Association
72 Main Street
P.O. Box 683
Sunapee, NH 03782
www.lakesunapee.org

The Lighthouse Inn
P.O. Box 128
1 Lighthouse Inn Road
West Dennis, MA 02670
www.lighthouseinn.com

The Lighthouse Kids
North Hampton School
201 Atlantic Ave.
North Hampton, NH 03862
www.lighthousekids.org

Lighthouse Preservation Society
4 Middle Street
Newburyport, MA 01950

Marshall Point Lighthouse Museum
P.O. Box 247
Port Clyde, ME 04855
www.marshallpoint.org

Martha's Vineyard Historical Society
P.O. Box 1310
Edgartown, MA 02539
www.marthasvineyardhistory.org

Monhegan Historical and Cultural Museum
Association
1 Lighthouse Hill
Monhegan Island, ME 04852
www.briegull.com/monhegan/museum.html

Museum at Portland Head Light
1000 Shore Road
Cape Elizabeth, ME 04107
www.portlandheadlight.com

Nauset Light Preservation Society
P.O. Box 941
Eastham, MA 02642
www.nausetlight.org

New England Lighthouse Lovers
P.O. Box 1626
Groton, CT 06340
www.nell.cc

New London Ledge Lighthouse Foundation
P.O. Box 855
New London, CT 06320

Norwalk Seaport Association
132 Water Street
South Norwalk, CT 06854
www.seaport.org

Pine Island Camp
Belgrade Lakes, ME 04918
www.pineisland.org

Project Gurnet and Bug Lights
P.O. Box 2167
Duxbury, MA 02331
www.buglight.org

Prudence Conservancy
P.O. Box 115
Prudence Island, RI 02872
www.prudenceconservancy.org

Ram Island Preservation Society
P.O. Box 123
Boothbay, ME 04537

The Range Light Keepers
79 Iron Mine Rd.
Arrowsic, ME 04530www.rlk.org

Rose Island Lighthouse Foundation
P.O. Box 1419
Newport, RI 02840
www.roseislandlighthouse.org

Scituate Historical Society
P.O. Box 276
Scituate, MA 02066
www.scituatehistoricalsociety.org

Shelburne Museum
U.S. Route 7, P.O. Box 10
Shelburne, VT 05482
www.shelburnemuseum.org

Spring Point Ledge Light Trust
P.O. Box 2311
South Portland, ME 04106
www.springpointlight.org

St. Croix Historical Society
P.O. Box 242
Calais, ME 04619

Stonington Historical Society
P.O. Box 103
Stonington, CT 06378
www.stoningtonhistory.org

Thacher Island Association
P.O. Box 73
Rockport, MA 01966
www.thacherisland.org

Watch Hill Lighthouse Keepers Association
14 Lighthouse Road
Watch Hill, RI 02891

West Quoddy Head Light Keepers Association
P.O. Box 378
Lubec, ME 04652
www.westquoddy.com

Winter Island Marine Recreational Park
50 Winter Island Road
Salem, MA 01970
www.salemweb.com/winterisland

Website References
www.lighthouse.cc
www.lhdigest.com
www.lighthousefoundation.org
www.cr.nps.gov/maritime/
www.acadiamagic.com

ACKNOWLEDGEMENTS

Twin Lights Publishers would like to thank the photographers whose love of New England's lighthouses shines so clearly through the images presented in this book. Their creative gift as photographers is what made this an exceptional keepsake. We would also like to thank lighthouse enthusiast Jeremy D'Entremont for his insight and willingness to share his in-depth knowledge of this area's lighthouses. Jeremy has researched and photographed lighthouses since the mid-1980's. He writes for *Lighthouse Digest Magazine* and his photographs have appeared in many magazines and other publications. Jeremy's assistance was invaluable. For more information on New England's lighthouses visit his website at www.lighthouse.cc.